Welcome to your Gymnastics Journal

This Gymnastics Journal Belongs To:

....

I am ....9... Years Old

My Date of Birth:

9-23-12

I Love Gymnastics Because:

I have friends and it is
fun.

Gymnastics Skill I am Most Proud of:

Kip on high bar + low
bar

My Gymnastics Goal:

To run faster on
vault.

Gymnastics Journal

Contents Page

Gymnastics Journal

All About Me

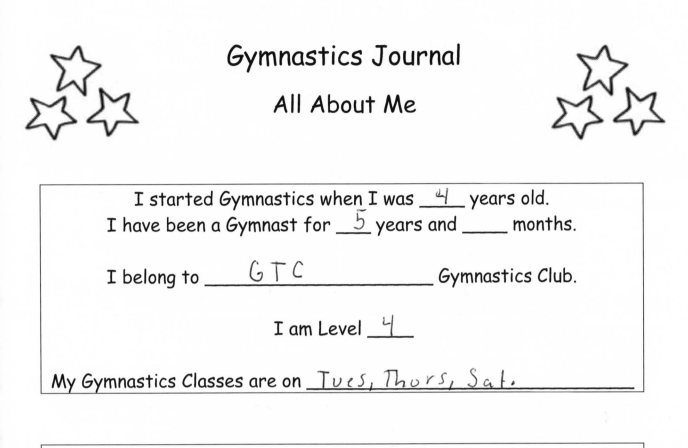

I started Gymnastics when I was __4__ years old.
I have been a Gymnast for __5__ years and _____ months.

I belong to ____GTC_____ Gymnastics Club.

I am Level __4__

My Gymnastics Classes are on __Tues, Thurs, Sat._____

My Favorite thing about Gymnastics is:

That I have friends and have fun.

My Favorite Moves are:

The Whole beam routine.

Gymnastics Journal
All About Me

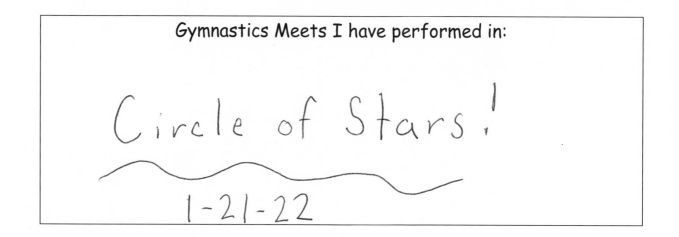

Gymnastics Meets I have performed in:

Circle of Stars!

1-21-22

My Most Challenging Events: bars

My Most Challenging Skill: roundoff bhs bhs

My Highest All-Round Score: 26.1

My Highest Event Score: beam

Future Goals in Gynastics: make high bar + low bar kip

Gymnastics Journal

All About Me

My Best Skills at the:

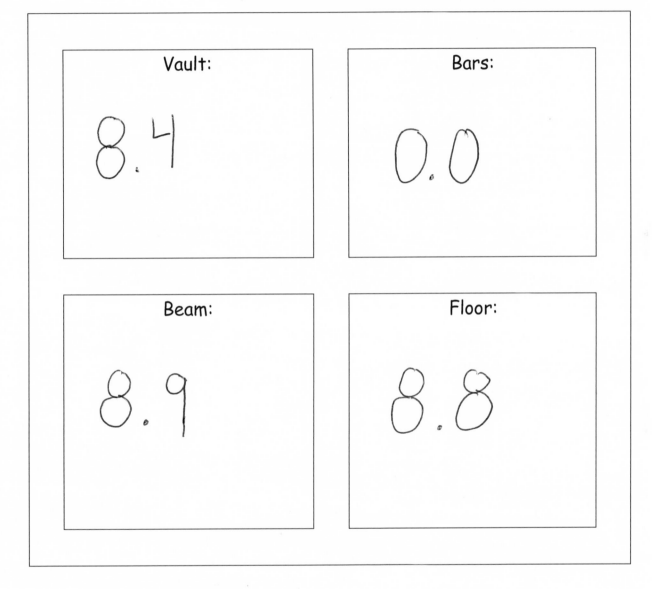

Vault:

8.4

Bars:

0.0

Beam:

8.9

Floor:

8.8

My Favorite Floor Music:

Level 4 music

Gymnastics Journal
My Coaches and Team

My Coaches:

My Favorite Coach is:

Because:

Best Coach Phrases:

My Coach always tells me to:

And I say:

Gymnastics Journal
My Coaches and Team

My Teammates:

My Best Team Friends:

Best Team Phrases:

As a Team we love to:

We Relax by:

My Dream Gymnastics Team would include:

Gymnastics Journal
Weekly Practice Notes

Date:

Main Goals for this week:

Vault Skills I have been working on:

Bar Skills I have been working on:

Beam Skills I have been working on:

Floor Skills I have been working on:

Floor Music:

Gymnastics Journal
Weekly Practice Notes

Reflection on Practice (complete before next practice):

What went well:

What I have found difficult or challenging:

Feedback from Coach or Teammates:

What I am Most proud of:

Look back at the Goals for this week......

Have any of these goals been achieved?

What can I do to try and achieve these goals?

Gymnastics Journal
Weekly Practice Notes

Date:

Main Goals for this week:

Vault Skills I have been working on:

Bar Skills I have been working on:

Beam Skills I have been working on:

Floor Skills I have been working on:

Floor Music:

Gymnastics Journal
Weekly Practice Notes

Reflection on Practice (complete before next practice):

What went well:

What I have found difficult or challenging:

Feedback from Coach or Teammates:

What I am Most proud of:

Look back at the Goals for this week......

Have any of these goals been achieved?

What can I do to try and achieve these goals?

Gymnastics Journal
Weekly Practice Notes

Date:

Main Goals for this week:

Vault Skills I have been working on:

Bar Skills I have been working on:

Beam Skills I have been working on:

Floor Skills I have been working on:

Floor Music:

Gymnastics Journal
Weekly Practice Notes

Reflection on Practice (complete before next practice):

What went well:

What I have found difficult or challenging:

Feedback from Coach or Teammates:

What I am Most proud of:

Look back at the Goals for this week......

Have any of these goals been achieved?

What can I do to try and achieve these goals?

Gymnastics Journal
Weekly Practice Notes

Date:

Main Goals for this week:

Vault Skills I have been working on:

Bar Skills I have been working on:

Beam Skills I have been working on:

Floor Skills I have been working on:

Floor Music:

Gymnastics Journal
Weekly Practice Notes

Reflection on Practice (complete before next practice):

What went well:

What I have found difficult or challenging:

Feedback from Coach or Teammates:

What I am Most proud of:

Look back at the Goals for this week......

Have any of these goals been achieved?

What can I do to try and achieve these goals?

Gymnastics Journal
Weekly Practice Notes

Date:

Main Goals for this week:

Vault Skills I have been working on:

Bar Skills I have been working on:

Beam Skills I have been working on:

Floor Skills I have been working on:

Floor Music:

Gymnastics Journal
Weekly Practice Notes

Reflection on Practice (complete before next practice):

What went well:

What I have found difficult or challenging:

Feedback from Coach or Teammates:

What I am Most proud of:

Look back at the Goals for this week......

Have any of these goals been achieved?

What can I do to try and achieve these goals?

Gymnastics Journal
Weekly Practice Notes

Date:

Main Goals for this week:

Vault Skills I have been working on:

Bar Skills I have been working on:

Beam Skills I have been working on:

Floor Skills I have been working on:

Floor Music:

Gymnastics Journal
Weekly Practice Notes

Reflection on Practice (complete before next practice):

What went well:

What I have found difficult or challenging:

Feedback from Coach or Teammates:

What I am Most proud of:

Look back at the Goals for this week……

Have any of these goals been achieved?

What can I do to try and achieve these goals?

Gymnastics Journal
Weekly Practice Notes

Date:

Main Goals for this week:

Vault Skills I have been working on:

Bar Skills I have been working on:

Beam Skills I have been working on:

Floor Skills I have been working on:

Floor Music:

Gymnastics Journal
Weekly Practice Notes

Reflection on Practice (complete before next practice):

What went well:

What I have found difficult or challenging:

Feedback from Coach or Teammates:

What I am Most proud of:

Look back at the Goals for this week......

Have any of these goals been achieved?

What can I do to try and achieve these goals?

 # Gymnastics Journal
Weekly Practice Notes

Date:

Main Goals for this week:

Vault Skills I have been working on:

Bar Skills I have been working on:

Beam Skills I have been working on:

Floor Skills I have been working on:

Floor Music:

Gymnastics Journal
Weekly Practice Notes

Reflection on Practice (complete before next practice):

What went well:

What I have found difficult or challenging:

Feedback from Coach or Teammates:

What I am Most proud of:

Look back at the Goals for this week......

Have any of these goals been achieved?

What can I do to try and achieve these goals?

Gymnastics Journal
Weekly Practice Notes

Date:

Main Goals for this week:

Vault Skills I have been working on:

Bar Skills I have been working on:

Beam Skills I have been working on:

Floor Skills I have been working on:

Floor Music:

Gymnastics Journal
Weekly Practice Notes

Reflection on Practice (complete before next practice):

What went well:

What I have found difficult or challenging:

Feedback from Coach or Teammates:

What I am Most proud of:

Look back at the Goals for this week……

Have any of these goals been achieved?

What can I do to try and achieve these goals?

Gymnastics Journal
Weekly Practice Notes

Date:

Main Goals for this week:

Vault Skills I have been working on:

Bar Skills I have been working on:

Beam Skills I have been working on:

Floor Skills I have been working on:

Floor Music:

 # Gymnastics Journal
Weekly Practice Notes

Reflection on Practice (complete before next practice):

What went well:

What I have found difficult or challenging:

Feedback from Coach or Teammates:

What I am Most proud of:

Look back at the Goals for this week......

Have any of these goals been achieved?

What can I do to try and achieve these goals?

 # Gymnastics Journal
Weekly Practice Notes

Date:

Main Goals for this week:

Vault Skills I have been working on:

Bar Skills I have been working on:

Beam Skills I have been working on:

Floor Skills I have been working on:

Floor Music:

Gymnastics Journal
Weekly Practice Notes

Reflection on Practice (complete before next practice):

What went well:

What I have found difficult or challenging:

Feedback from Coach or Teammates:

What I am Most proud of:

Look back at the Goals for this week......

Have any of these goals been achieved?

What can I do to try and achieve these goals?

Gymnastics Journal
Weekly Practice Notes

Date:

Main Goals for this week:

Vault Skills I have been working on:

Bar Skills I have been working on:

Beam Skills I have been working on:

Floor Skills I have been working on:

Floor Music:

Gymnastics Journal
Weekly Practice Notes

Reflection on Practice (complete before next practice):

What went well:

What I have found difficult or challenging:

Feedback from Coach or Teammates:

What I am Most proud of:

Look back at the Goals for this week......

Have any of these goals been achieved?

What can I do to try and achieve these goals?

 # Gymnastics Journal
Weekly Practice Notes

Date:

Main Goals for this week:

Vault Skills I have been working on:

Bar Skills I have been working on:

Beam Skills I have been working on:

Floor Skills I have been working on:

Floor Music:

Gymnastics Journal
Weekly Practice Notes

Reflection on Practice (complete before next practice):

What went well:

What I have found difficult or challenging:

Feedback from Coach or Teammates:

What I am Most proud of:

Look back at the Goals for this week......

Have any of these goals been achieved?

What can I do to try and achieve these goals?

Gymnastics Journal
Weekly Practice Notes

Date:

Main Goals for this week:

Vault Skills I have been working on:

Bar Skills I have been working on:

Beam Skills I have been working on:

Floor Skills I have been working on:

Floor Music:

Gymnastics Journal
Weekly Practice Notes

Reflection on Practice (complete before next practice):

What went well:

What I have found difficult or challenging:

Feedback from Coach or Teammates:

What I am Most proud of:

Look back at the Goals for this week......

Have any of these goals been achieved?

What can I do to try and achieve these goals?

Gymnastics Journal
Weekly Practice Notes

Date:

Main Goals for this week:

Vault Skills I have been working on:

Bar Skills I have been working on:

Beam Skills I have been working on:

Floor Skills I have been working on:

Floor Music:

Gymnastics Journal
Weekly Practice Notes

Reflection on Practice (complete before next practice):

What went well:

What I have found difficult or challenging:

Feedback from Coach or Teammates:

What I am Most proud of:

Look back at the Goals for this week......

Have any of these goals been achieved?

What can I do to try and achieve these goals?

 # Gymnastics Journal
Weekly Practice Notes

Date:

Main Goals for this week:

Vault Skills I have been working on:

Bar Skills I have been working on:

Beam Skills I have been working on:

Floor Skills I have been working on:

Floor Music:

Gymnastics Journal
Weekly Practice Notes

Reflection on Practice (complete before next practice):

What went well:

What I have found difficult or challenging:

Feedback from Coach or Teammates:

What I am Most proud of:

Look back at the Goals for this week......

Have any of these goals been achieved?

What can I do to try and achieve these goals?

Gymnastics Journal
Weekly Practice Notes

Date:

Main Goals for this week:

Vault Skills I have been working on:

Bar Skills I have been working on:

Beam Skills I have been working on:

Floor Skills I have been working on:

Floor Music:

Gymnastics Journal
Weekly Practice Notes

Reflection on Practice (complete before next practice):

What went well:

What I have found difficult or challenging:

Feedback from Coach or Teammates:

What I am Most proud of:

Look back at the Goals for this week……

Have any of these goals been achieved?

What can I do to try and achieve these goals?

 # Gymnastics Journal
Weekly Practice Notes

Date:

Main Goals for this week:

Vault Skills I have been working on:

Bar Skills I have been working on:

Beam Skills I have been working on:

Floor Skills I have been working on:

Floor Music:

Gymnastics Journal
Weekly Practice Notes

Reflection on Practice (complete before next practice):

What went well:

What I have found difficult or challenging:

Feedback from Coach or Teammates:

What I am Most proud of:

Look back at the Goals for this week……

Have any of these goals been achieved?

What can I do to try and achieve these goals?

Gymnastics Journal
Weekly Practice Notes

Date:

Main Goals for this week:

Vault Skills I have been working on:

Bar Skills I have been working on:

Beam Skills I have been working on:

Floor Skills I have been working on:

Floor Music:

Gymnastics Journal
Weekly Practice Notes

Reflection on Practice (complete before next practice):

What went well:

What I have found difficult or challenging:

Feedback from Coach or Teammates:

What I am Most proud of:

Look back at the Goals for this week......

Have any of these goals been achieved?

What can I do to try and achieve these goals?

Gymnastics Journal
Weekly Practice Notes

Date:

Main Goals for this week:

Vault Skills I have been working on:

Bar Skills I have been working on:

Beam Skills I have been working on:

Floor Skills I have been working on:

Floor Music:

Gymnastics Journal
Weekly Practice Notes

Reflection on Practice (complete before next practice):

What went well:

What I have found difficult or challenging:

Feedback from Coach or Teammates:

What I am Most proud of:

Look back at the Goals for this week......

Have any of these goals been achieved?

What can I do to try and achieve these goals?

Gymnastics Journal
Weekly Practice Notes

Date:

Main Goals for this week:

Vault Skills I have been working on:

Bar Skills I have been working on:

Beam Skills I have been working on:

Floor Skills I have been working on:

Floor Music:

Gymnastics Journal
Weekly Practice Notes

Reflection on Practice (complete before next practice):

What went well:

What I have found difficult or challenging:

Feedback from Coach or Teammates:

What I am Most proud of:

Look back at the Goals for this week......

Have any of these goals been achieved?

What can I do to try and achieve these goals?

Gymnastics Journal
Weekly Practice Notes

Date:

Main Goals for this week:

Vault Skills I have been working on:

Bar Skills I have been working on:

Beam Skills I have been working on:

Floor Skills I have been working on:

Floor Music:

Gymnastics Journal
Weekly Practice Notes

Reflection on Practice (complete before next practice):

What went well:

What I have found difficult or challenging:

Feedback from Coach or Teammates:

What I am Most proud of:

Look back at the Goals for this week……

Have any of these goals been achieved?

What can I do to try and achieve these goals?

Gymnastics Journal
Weekly Practice Notes

Date:

Main Goals for this week:

Vault Skills I have been working on:

Bar Skills I have been working on:

Beam Skills I have been working on:

Floor Skills I have been working on:

Floor Music:

Gymnastics Journal
Weekly Practice Notes

Reflection on Practice (complete before next practice):

What went well:

What I have found difficult or challenging:

Feedback from Coach or Teammates:

What I am Most proud of:

Look back at the Goals for this week......

Have any of these goals been achieved?

What can I do to try and achieve these goals?

Gymnastics Journal
Weekly Practice Notes

Date:

Main Goals for this week:

Vault Skills I have been working on:

Bar Skills I have been working on:

Beam Skills I have been working on:

Floor Skills I have been working on:

Floor Music:

Gymnastics Journal
Weekly Practice Notes

Reflection on Practice (complete before next practice):

What went well:

What I have found difficult or challenging:

Feedback from Coach or Teammates:

What I am Most proud of:

Look back at the Goals for this week......

Have any of these goals been achieved?

What can I do to try and achieve these goals?

Gymnastics Journal
Weekly Practice Notes

Date:

Main Goals for this week:

Vault Skills I have been working on:

Bar Skills I have been working on:

Beam Skills I have been working on:

Floor Skills I have been working on:

Floor Music:

Gymnastics Journal
Weekly Practice Notes

Reflection on Practice (complete before next practice):

What went well:

What I have found difficult or challenging:

Feedback from Coach or Teammates:

What I am Most proud of:

Look back at the Goals for this week......

Have any of these goals been achieved?

What can I do to try and achieve these goals?

Gymnastics Journal
Weekly Practice Notes

Date:

Main Goals for this week:

Vault Skills I have been working on:

Bar Skills I have been working on:

Beam Skills I have been working on:

Floor Skills I have been working on:

Floor Music:

Gymnastics Journal
Weekly Practice Notes

Reflection on Practice (complete before next practice):

What went well:

What I have found difficult or challenging:

Feedback from Coach or Teammates:

What I am Most proud of:

Look back at the Goals for this week......

Have any of these goals been achieved?

What can I do to try and achieve these goals?

Gymnastics Journal
Competition Check List

Be Prepared for your next Gymnastics Competition -

What helps me to relax?

What helps me to focus?

Things to do Before the Competition (tick when complete):

1. _____

   _____ ☐

2. _____

   _____ ☐

3. _____

   _____ ☐

4. _____

   _____ ☐

5. _____

   _____ ☐

6. _____

   _____ ☐

Gymnastics Journal
Competition Check List

Be Prepared for your next Gymnastics Competition -

What helps me to relax?

What helps me to focus?

Things to do Before the Competition (tick when complete):

1. _____ ☐

_____

2. _____ ☐

_____

3. _____ ☐

_____

4. _____ ☐

_____

5. _____ ☐

_____

6. _____ ☐

_____

Gymnastics Journal
Competition Check List

Be Prepared for your next Gymnastics Competition -

What helps me to relax?

What helps me to focus?

Things to do Before the Competition (tick when complete):

1. _____ ☐

_____

2. _____ ☐

_____

3. _____ ☐

_____

4. _____ ☐

_____

5. _____ ☐

_____

6. _____ ☐

_____

Gymnastics Journal
Competition Check List

Be Prepared for your next Gymnastics Competition -

What helps me to relax?

What helps me to focus?

Things to do Before the Competition (tick when complete):

1. _____ ☐

_____

2. _____ ☐

_____

3. _____ ☐

_____

4. _____ ☐

_____

5. _____ ☐

_____

6. _____ ☐

_____

Gymnastics Journal
Competition Check List

Be Prepared for your next Gymnastics Competition -

What helps me to relax?

What helps me to focus?

Things to do Before the Competition (tick when complete):

1. _____ ☐
_____

2. _____ ☐
_____

3. _____ ☐
_____

4. _____ ☐
_____

5. _____ ☐
_____

6. _____ ☐
_____

Gymnastics Journal
Competition Check List

Be Prepared for your next Gymnastics Competition -

What helps me to relax?

What helps me to focus?

Things to do Before the Competition (tick when complete):

1. _____
   _____ ☐

2. _____
   _____ ☐

3. _____
   _____ ☐

4. _____
   _____ ☐

5. _____
   _____ ☐

6. _____
   _____ ☐

Gymnastics Journal
Competition Check List

Be Prepared for your next Gymnastics Competition -

What helps me to relax?

What helps me to focus?

Things to do Before the Competition (tick when complete):

1. _____
   _____ ☐

2. _____
   _____ ☐

3. _____
   _____ ☐

4. _____
   _____ ☐

5. _____
   _____ ☐

6. _____
   _____ ☐

Gymnastics Journal
Competition Check List

Be Prepared for your next Gymnastics Competition -

What helps me to relax?

What helps me to focus?

Things to do Before the Competition (tick when complete):

1. _____

   _____ ☐

2. _____

   _____ ☐

3. _____

   _____ ☐

4. _____

   _____ ☐

5. _____

   _____ ☐

6. _____

   _____ ☐

Gymnastics Journal
Competition Check List

Be Prepared for your next Gymnastics Competition -

What helps me to relax?

What helps me to focus?

Things to do Before the Competition (tick when complete):

1. _____ ☐

2. _____ ☐

3. _____ ☐

4. _____ ☐

5. _____ ☐

6. _____ ☐

Gymnastics Journal
Competition Check List

Be Prepared for your next Gymnastics Competition -

What helps me to relax?

What helps me to focus?

Things to do Before the Competition (tick when complete):

1. _____
   _____ ☐

2. _____
   _____ ☐

3. _____
   _____ ☐

4. _____
   _____ ☐

5. _____
   _____ ☐

6. _____
   _____ ☐

Gymnastics Journal
Meets / Competitions

Meet: Cupid Classic

Date: 2-5-22

Level: 4

Location: Dyer

Age Division: 9 - 11

Vault: O	Bars:
Score: 8.6 Position:	Score: 8.175 Position:
Beam:	Floor:
Score: 9.4.25 Position: 2nd	Score: 9.175 Position: 3rd

Overall Performance:

Score: 35.375

Position:

Gymnastics Journal
Meets / Competitions

Team Performance:

Team Score: Team Position:

Rate this Meet: ☆☆☆☆☆

At this Meet, I am Most Proud of:

I am Feeling:

Best Moments:

Worst Moments:

What I need to work on:

Feedback / Comments from Coach and Teammates:

Gymnastics Journal
Meets / Competitions

Meet:

Date: Location:

Level: Age Division:

Vault:

Score:
Position:

Bars:

Score:
Position:

Beam:

Score:
Position:

Floor:

Score:
Position:

Overall Performance:

Score: Position:

Gymnastics Journal
Meets / Competitions

Team Performance:

Team Score: Team Position:

Rate this Meet: ☆☆☆☆☆

At this Meet, I am Most Proud of:

I am Feeling:

Best Moments:

Worst Moments:

What I need to work on:

Feedback / Comments from Coach and Teammates:

Gymnastics Journal
Meets / Competitions

Meet:

Date: Location:

Level: Age Division:

Vault:	Bars:
Score: Position:	Score: Position:
Beam:	Floor:
Score: Position:	Score: Position:

Overall Performance:

Score: Position:

Gymnastics Journal
Meets / Competitions

Team Performance:

Team Score: Team Position:

Rate this Meet: ☆☆☆☆☆

At this Meet, I am Most Proud of:

I am Feeling:

Best Moments:

Worst Moments:

What I need to work on:

Feedback / Comments from Coach and Teammates:

Gymnastics Journal
Meets / Competitions

Meet:

Date: Location:

Level: Age Division:

Vault:

Score:
Position:

Bars:

Score:
Position:

Beam:

Score:
Position:

Floor:

Score:
Position:

Overall Performance:

Score: Position:

Gymnastics Journal
Meets / Competitions

Team Performance:

Team Score:

Team Position:

Rate this Meet: ☆☆☆☆☆

At this Meet, I am Most Proud of:

I am Feeling:

Best Moments:

Worst Moments:

What I need to work on:

Feedback / Comments from Coach and Teammates:

Gymnastics Journal
Meets / Competitions

Meet:

Date: Location:

Level: Age Division:

Vault:	Bars:
Score: Position:	Score: Position:
Beam:	Floor:
Score: Position:	Score: Position:

Overall Performance:

Score: Position:

Gymnastics Journal
Meets / Competitions

Team Performance:

Team Score: _____   Team Position: _____

Rate this Meet: ☆☆☆☆☆

At this Meet, I am Most Proud of:

I am Feeling:

Best Moments:

Worst Moments:

What I need to work on:

Feedback / Comments from Coach and Teammates:

Gymnastics Journal
Meets / Competitions

Meet:

Date: Location:

Level: Age Division:

Vault:

Score:
Position:

Bars:

Score:
Position:

Beam:

Score:
Position:

Floor:

Score:
Position:

Overall Performance:

Score: Position:

Gymnastics Journal
Meets / Competitions

Team Performance:

Team Score: Team Position:

Rate this Meet: ☆☆☆☆☆

At this Meet, I am Most Proud of:

I am Feeling:

Best Moments:

Worst Moments:

What I need to work on:

Feedback / Comments from Coach and Teammates:

Gymnastics Journal
Meets / Competitions

Meet:

Date: Location:

Level: Age Division:

Vault:	Bars:
Score: Position:	Score: Position:
Beam:	**Floor:**
Score: Position:	Score: Position:

Overall Performance:

Score: Position:

Gymnastics Journal
Meets / Competitions

Team Performance:

Team Score: Team Position:

Rate this Meet: ☆☆☆☆☆

At this Meet, I am Most Proud of:

I am Feeling:

Best Moments:

Worst Moments:

What I need to work on:

Feedback / Comments from Coach and Teammates:

Gymnastics Journal
Meets / Competitions

Meet:

Date:

Level:

Location:

Age Division:

Vault:	Bars:
Score: Position:	Score: Position:
Beam:	Floor:
Score: Position:	Score: Position:

Overall Performance:

Score: Position:

Gymnastics Journal
Meets / Competitions

Team Performance:

Team Score:

Team Position:

Rate this Meet: ☆☆☆☆☆

At this Meet, I am Most Proud of:

I am Feeling:

Best Moments:

Worst Moments:

What I need to work on:

Feedback / Comments from Coach and Teammates:

Gymnastics Journal
Meets / Competitions

Meet:

Date: Location:

Level: Age Division:

Vault:

Score:
Position:

Bars:

Score:
Position:

Beam:

Score:
Position:

Floor:

Score:
Position:

Overall Performance:

Score: Position:

Gymnastics Journal
Meets / Competitions

Team Performance:

Team Score: Team Position:

Rate this Meet: ☆☆☆☆☆

At this Meet, I am Most Proud of:

I am Feeling:

Best Moments:

Worst Moments:

What I need to work on:

Feedback / Comments from Coach and Teammates:

Gymnastics Journal
Meets / Competitions

Meet:

Date: Location:

Level: Age Division:

Vault:	Bars:
Score: Position:	Score: Position:
Beam:	Floor:
Score: Position:	Score: Position:

Overall Performance:

Score: Position:

Gymnastics Journal
Meets / Competitions

Team Performance:

Team Score: Team Position:

Rate this Meet: ☆☆☆☆☆

At this Meet, I am Most Proud of:

I am Feeling:

Best Moments:

Worst Moments:

What I need to work on:

Feedback / Comments from Coach and Teammates:

Gymnastics Journal
Setting Goals

Dream Goal:

How can I achieve this Goal?

When do I hope to achieve this Goal?

Review this Goal: (Date)

What Steps have I made to achieve this Goal?

Tick if Goal Complete: ☐

Long Term Goal:

How can I achieve this Goal?

When do I hope to achieve this Goal?

Review this Goal: (Date)

What Steps have I made to achieve this Goal?

Tick if Goal Complete: ☐

Gymnastics Journal
Setting Goals

Medium Term Goal:

How can I achieve this Goal?

When do I hope to achieve this Goal?

Review this Goal: (Date)

What Steps have I made to achieve this Goal?

Tick if Goal Complete: ☐

Medium Term Goal:

How can I achieve this Goal?

When do I hope to achieve this Goal?

Review this Goal: (Date)

What Steps have I made to achieve this Goal?

Tick if Goal Complete: ☐

Gymnastics Journal
Setting Goals

Medium Term Goal:

How can I achieve this Goal?

When do I hope to achieve this Goal?

Review this Goal: (Date)

What Steps have I made to achieve this Goal?

Tick if Goal Complete: ☐

Medium Term Goal:

How can I achieve this Goal?

When do I hope to achieve this Goal?

Review this Goal: (Date)

What Steps have I made to achieve this Goal?

Tick if Goal Complete: ☐

Gymnastics Journal
Setting Goals

Medium Term Goal:

How can I achieve this Goal?

When do I hope to achieve this Goal?

Review this Goal: (Date)

What Steps have I made to achieve this Goal?

Tick if Goal Complete: ☐

Medium Term Goal:

How can I achieve this Goal?

When do I hope to achieve this Goal?

Review this Goal: (Date)

What Steps have I made to achieve this Goal?

Tick if Goal Complete: ☐

Gymnastics Journal
Setting Goals

Medium Term Goal:

How can I achieve this Goal?

When do I hope to achieve this Goal?

Review this Goal: (Date)

What Steps have I made to achieve this Goal?

Tick if Goal Complete: ☐

Medium Term Goal:

How can I achieve this Goal?

When do I hope to achieve this Goal?

Review this Goal: (Date)

What Steps have I made to achieve this Goal?

Tick if Goal Complete: ☐

Gymnastics Journal
Setting Goals

Short Term Goal:

How can I achieve this Goal?

When do I hope to achieve this Goal?

Review this Goal: (Date)

What Steps have I made to achieve this Goal?

Tick if Goal Complete: ☐

Short Term Goal:

How can I achieve this Goal?

When do I hope to achieve this Goal?

Review this Goal: (Date)

What Steps have I made to achieve this Goal?

Tick if Goal Complete: ☐

 # Gymnastics Journal
Setting Goals

Short Term Goal:

How can I achieve this Goal?

When do I hope to achieve this Goal?

Review this Goal: (Date)

What Steps have I made to achieve this Goal?

Tick if Goal Complete: ☐

Short Term Goal:

How can I achieve this Goal?

When do I hope to achieve this Goal?

Review this Goal: (Date)

What Steps have I made to achieve this Goal?

Tick if Goal Complete: ☐

Gymnastics Journal
Setting Goals

Short Term Goal:

How can I achieve this Goal?

When do I hope to achieve this Goal?

Review this Goal: (Date)

What Steps have I made to achieve this Goal?

Tick if Goal Complete: ☐

Short Term Goal:

How can I achieve this Goal?

When do I hope to achieve this Goal?

Review this Goal: (Date)

What Steps have I made to achieve this Goal?

Tick if Goal Complete: ☐

Gymnastics Journal
Setting Goals

Short Term Goal:

How can I achieve this Goal?

When do I hope to achieve this Goal?

Review this Goal: (Date)

What Steps have I made to achieve this Goal?

Tick if Goal Complete: ☐

Short Term Goal:

How can I achieve this Goal?

When do I hope to achieve this Goal?

Review this Goal: (Date)

What Steps have I made to achieve this Goal?

Tick if Goal Complete: ☐

Gymnastics Journal
Setting Goals

Short Term Goal:

How can I achieve this Goal?

When do I hope to achieve this Goal?

Review this Goal: (Date)

What Steps have I made to achieve this Goal?

Tick if Goal Complete: ☐

Short Term Goal:

How can I achieve this Goal?

When do I hope to achieve this Goal?

Review this Goal: (Date)

What Steps have I made to achieve this Goal?

Tick if Goal Complete: ☐

Gymnastics Journal
General Notes

_____
_____
_____
_____
_____
_____
_____
_____
_____
_____
_____
_____
_____
_____
_____
_____
_____
_____
_____
_____

Gymnastics Journal
General Notes

_____

_____

_____

_____

_____

_____

_____

_____

_____

_____

_____

_____

_____

_____

_____

_____

_____

_____

_____

_____

_____

_____

_____

Gymnastics Journal
General Notes

Gymnastics Journal
General Notes

Gymnastics Journal
General Notes

Gymnastics Journal
General Notes

Gymnastics Journal
General Notes

_____

_____

_____

_____

_____

_____

_____

_____

_____

_____

_____

_____

_____

_____

_____

_____

_____

_____

_____

_____

_____

Gymnastics Journal
General Notes

Gymnastics Journal
General Notes

Gymnastics Journal
General Notes

Gymnastics Journal
General Notes

 # Gymnastics Journal
Thank You

Thank you so much for using this Gymnastics Journal. I hope you have found it useful and that it has helped you make progress in your Gymnastics.

I would be grateful if you could leave a review of this Journal on Amazon.

Go to Amazon and type in the name of this Journal:

"Gymnastics Journal" by Freya Carter.

Scroll down till you see 'Leave Review'.

Let me know what you think. I look forward to hearing from you and I really appreciate your time.

Best Wishes and all the very best with your Gymnastics.

Freya Carter

Made in the USA
Monee, IL
11 December 2021